Our Story with God

Our Story with God

by Magdalena Dodds

Our Story With God
Copyright ©2021 Magdalena Dodds

All rights reserved. This book or any portion thereof may not be reproduced or used in any manner whatsoever without the express written permission of the publisher except for the use of brief quotations in a book review.

Published by:
Spring of Hope Foundation, Inc.
P.O. Box 100348
San Antonio, TX 78201

ISBN: 979-8-218-02302-7

Editor: Lillie Ammann
Cover Designer: Cynthia Lee
Interior Layout: Jan McClintock

Dedication

Dedicated to the memory of my beloved husband,
Ron Dodds, Jr.
and our life together with God.

Preface

Why Write this Book?

The main story revolves around Ron Dodds, Jr, who was an extraordinary warrior for Christ. However, I do not want to paint him as a perfect person because he was not. He had flaws just like any human being. He was born in Pottsville, Pennsylvania, and his family moved to Florida when he and his sister were school age. He suffered some hardship, but in hearing all of his stories, it seemed to me that he had favor with God.

He and his sister were blessed to be extremely intelligent. He had a great sense of humor that could defuse any situation. I remember him telling me that sometimes things came too easily to him. He was a great athlete and had a photographic memory, which he said could be a blessing and a curse. He served in the military for a short time.

After that, when he was struggling, he was hired by a family in Melbourne, Florida, to work in their business. I am sure he was very successful because in our marriage, he was an excellent businessman. I used to call him "the moneymaker." It didn't matter what he touched, he seemed to be able to make money at it. The family that hired him also adopted him; he attended their church, and that is how he got saved. He was introduced to Jewish Messianic ministry, and he developed a love for Israel.

I would like to say that this book is about Ron, but it is not. I am hoping as you read these pages that you can see that it was never about him or about our life together. It was all about what God did for us and how He created miracles time after time. There is a song by Big Daddy Weave that says, "Oh to tell you my story, is to tell of Him." That is exactly what I would like you to see as you read the pages.

After Ron and I both dedicated our lives to God and went into ministry, it became all about Jesus. My prayer as you read what God did in our lives is that you would be encouraged and realize that He will do the same for you. Life with the Lord is not always easy. However, He always makes a way, even in the midst of the most difficult times.

Chapter 1

A Chance Meeting

How do I begin to tell the story of my life? I won't start at the very beginning, but I will start at the beginning of what came to be the most important period of my life.

I was working at a graphics company as an accountant. It was the first job I had where I was using my degree. The company was out of Kansas City, Kansas. The business flew me to Kansas for my second interview. I had never flown before. I remember flying from San Antonio to Houston. I don't even remember which airport in Houston I flew out of, but what I do remember is that I had to take a tram from one terminal to the next to catch my flight.

Here I was in a two-piece skirt suit and a briefcase (remember briefcases?). When the tram arrived, there was no one in it and no one driving it! I jumped in, looking silly, I'm sure. I arrived in Kansas City and interviewed with the controller, who loved me. He told me that I would have to train in Kansas City for two weeks. So, I drove from my home in Texas to Kansas City. I went on the long drive for the first time in my life. It was long, boring, and very flat.

However, I clicked with the team in Kansas City. It was the first time that I had lived away from home for any length of time, so I cried at night because I missed my family. I was very homesick. However, the team took me to different places.

On one occasion, a fellow accountant took me to the Renaissance Festival. It was during the fall and the trees had changed color. The trees were so tall compared to Texas trees. It was almost like I went back in time. It was all so beautiful. After I finished my training, I went back to San Antonio and started my job there. Three months later, in January, my life changed forever.

The company hired a man named Ron for the position of technical director. He came on full time managing a team. The first time I met him, he wore a suit. I happened to be passing by and the general manager introduced us.

Since I also handled payroll, I asked Ron to submit the necessary forms so I could set him up in the system. He responded, "I am very busy this week, but I'll submit it to you by the end of the week." I remember turning around and thinking "Oh, wonderful. They hired another jerk in this company!" I just thought he was the most arrogant person that I had ever met.

My disdain did not last too long because my keyboard broke later that week and Ron came to my office to troubleshoot it. He was very different from my first impression. He was very funny and made me laugh.

That day for a split second, I thought, *I could spend the rest of my life with him,* which was a very odd thought because I had resigned myself to never getting married. Although it was not a serious relationship, I was dating another man in the office. He was much younger than me, but he was fun to hang around with.

Ron and I started going to lunch on a regular basis. We became friends. He flirted with all the girls in the office except with me. I discovered that our birthdays were very close together; my birthday was July 18 and Ron's was July 16. I mentioned this detail to him, and I suggested that we go out for dinner on July 17 to celebrate our birthdays. He agreed.

I was still dating another young man so on July 16, this other young man took me to a movie. He wore shorts and brought me carnations. It was a very casual date.

The next day, Ron took me out on our agreed upon "date" and he wore a suit. He gave me roses and took me to Ruth's Chris for dinner. During dinner I told him that I was dating that other young man, who was also a friend of his. Ron said that I was "pathetic." We went to the Riverwalk and enjoyed the sights.

Later that evening, Ron expressed his love for me, and I didn't know what to do with that. I liked him fine as a friend, but at the time I didn't have any romantic feelings toward him. He was from Florida, so I figured he was just lonely. In terms of dates though, that other young man was just a boy and Ron was a mature man.

Ron and I continued to talk on the phone and have our lunches. One day in August of 1993, I remember that he made an off-color joke regarding Hispanics, and I became angry with him. I was mad enough that I stopped speaking to him for about a month.

Something weird occurred though. I missed his friendship. We used to go to lunch all the time. I would pass by him at work and would feel my heart leap. One day late in August, I was invited to play pool with several employees. Initially, I had chosen not to attend because I knew Ron would there. He had one of his friends call me to convince me to attend. By this time, the other young man had broken up with me because he thought our relationship was getting too deep.

So I went to the get-together, and Ron started to talk to me. We talked until late, and again he professed that he wanted to date. Have you ever had a choice in front of you and known that God is giving you another chance? I felt as if I was in the middle of a crossroads and if I chose badly, I would miss out. I knew that I could not pass this up. So this time, I agreed to date.

God made me fall head over heels in love with him. I couldn't think at work. The only thing I could think of was Ron. We talked into the wee hours of the morning. We were on the phone as we each watched *Seinfeld*. He had roses delivered to my office every week. He took me on dates to nice restaurants.

On our second date, we went walking at a park, and he asked me if I thought I was going to heaven or if I was going to hell. I recognized that I was wicked inside, so I answered that I was going to hell.

He told me that it didn't have to be that way. I'm sure that I gave him a strange look, so he did not continue. I really thought that it was the oddest question anyone had ever asked me on a date.

One night in September or October, we arrived at my house where I lived with my sister and my son. Ron and I took a walk down the street, and he started asking me about the possibility of marrying him. I turned him down because there were too many differences between us. He proceeded like a salesman to discuss each topic and why it would not be a problem. By the end of the night, I agreed to marry him. Later, I would joke that the only reason I accepted was because I was tired and wanted to get some sleep.

Chapter 2

Marriage

On November 12, 1993, I married Ron. It was a small wedding with only my immediate family in attendance. Jerry, the general manager for the company that we worked for, was Ron's best man. They were good friends.

We spent our honeymoon in New Braunfels, just north of San Antonio. It's a quaint little German town. We thought that we could stay local then go to Cabo San Lucas at some point later.

I ended up looking for another job because the owner of the company did not want me to divulge payroll information to Ron. It would be a conflict of interest. I went to work as an accountant for an investment company. It turned out to be a good move for me. The business had great benefits, and through the next few years, I was able to move up in the company.

It was a good thing that we never took that big honeymoon trip because unfortunately Ron was laid off from the company where we'd met. Technology was changing, and the company was losing customers. Ron was dejected but soon found work in Austin, north of San Antonio. He was a graphic artist for a large printing company. The company paid well, but the hours were grueling. He worked a night shift, and he commuted an hour and half each way every day. It took a toll on our new marriage.

My son, Dorian, was reaching the teenage years and needed attention. Being married had its perks. Ron was an excellent leader and helped me make decisions that for so long I had made on my own. In reality, when we married, I didn't really know who Ron was, and I didn't recognize his potential. I just knew that I was madly in love with him.

After a year of struggling with him being gone so much, I asked him to find work closer to home because I knew that if he didn't, we just weren't going to make it. So, he found work, again as a graphic artist, in Boerne. It was also north of San Antonio, but closer than Austin; that commute was doable.

I had studied for the Certified Public Account (CPA) exam before and failed it. Ron asked me if this was important to me and if I really wanted to pursue it, and I said yes. He organized our household so that my sister, Evelyn, did many household tasks I had been doing. She was ten years younger than me and still lived with me and my twelve-year-old son.

Ron purchased a computer for me and every night for the next six months, I studied. I took the exam again and passed two parts. At that time, you had to take all four of the parts and pass at least fifty percent of them before moving forward. I passed the next two parts, and I was on my way to officially becoming a CPA. It was a great accomplishment for me, but one that I could not have achieved without Ron's leadership and support.

For the first year of our marriage, Ron attended Catholic church with my sister, son, and me. Ron asked me if I was interested in attending another type of church. He wanted a more Bible-based church.

I told him that I was open to visiting other churches. I had attended a Catholic college where in one of my classes, the instructor asked us to attend other churches as part of our class. Ron and I started attending a Baptist church where the pastor was a very prominent leader in the community. I certainly heard the salvation message during that year, but I don't think that I understood it all.

Chapter 3

Path to God

We moved into the house that I owned with my sister. We had built it in a new neighborhood on the Northeast side of town. It definitely served its purpose. At the time, Evelyn was going to college and working. She decided to move out on her own. I know it was difficult for her (and probably Dorian too) to see me married and for someone else to live in the house. Evelyn needed her own space.

The first years of our marriage were difficult because our son was on his way to becoming an adult and fell in with the wrong crowd. Prior to our marriage, Ron and I had each lived on our own, so we were pretty set in our ways. We disagreed a lot because we were trying to get used to living with one another.

One day around Christmas in late 1995, Ron and I were shopping at a store called MacFrugals. He saw a bumper sticker that said, "Pray for the Peace of Jerusalem." He inquired of the passenger where they got the sticker, but the woman in the car said that the vehicle belonged to her daughter, who was inside the store shopping. Ron had been involved with Messianic Jewish ministries when he lived in Florida, and he was hoping to find a similar type of church in San Antonio.

While we were shopping, an attractive woman came up to us and asked if we were inquiring about her bumper sticker. Because it was close to Christmas, the store was busy. I wondered how in the world she found us in that crowded store. We answered that we were searching for the right church.

She attended a Messianic Jewish church in San Antonio and invited us to visit. We attended in December of 1995, and I remember thinking it was the oddest service I had ever seen. People danced in the aisles and other people wore prayer shawls. I was very confused, but because I loved my husband, I continued to attend every Friday night.

One night in January of 1996, I remember hearing a particular song that was written and sung by the worship leader. That night the worship team sang that song; it went straight to my heart, and I started to cry uncontrollably.

I talked to Ron about it, and he said that we would pray about it when we got home. At home, we prayed, and I gave my life to the Lord Jesus Christ. In addition, the Lord gave me a love for Israel and the Jewish people.

My conversion was similar to that of the Apostle Paul, because scales fell from my eyes, and I saw the world for the first time in my life. It was like when Neo had to decide between the red and the blue pill in the movie *The Matrix*. I realized that I had been living a lie all of these years. It made me a bit sad because I was thirty-five years old when I gave my life to Jesus. I remember thinking that I had wasted so much time. I saw things from a whole new perspective.

Ron and I became active in the Messianic Jewish church. He started leading the youth ministry and had a unique group of students who were very intelligent, just like he was. He had a great rapport with them. Ron had a student named Isaac who would later become a great friend and even a mentor.

One of the elder's wives took an interest in me, and I started serving as a nursery leader. Everything I learned about serving in the church, I learned from her.

Evelyn and Dorian also were attending church with us. My sister was having a terrible time with her roommate, and Ron invited her to move back into our house—but not before he led her to the Lord. She gave her life to Christ. My son was a junior in high school, and he, too, surrendered his life to the Lord. Ron's family in Florida gave their lives to Christ one by one. Evelyn was dating my future brother-in-law, Kenneth, and he also committed his life to Christ.

We all fell like dominos—all because of the faith of my husband. He shared the Gospel, and he was a living example. The Lord is faithful when you give your life to him. It was a miracle that so many of our family members gave their lives to Christ.

Later, Ron would tell the story of how he had prayed for a wife and the Lord led him to Texas. He said that the first time he heard my voice, he knew he would marry me. He wanted to marry a believer, but he had faith that God would work it all out.

Really, when I think about this, I recognize it was a miracle that we came together. One wrong move and our destinies would have been very different. That demonstrates that God is an amazing God. He lets us make mistakes and follow our different paths until we are ready to turn to him. I feel so blessed that for whatever reason, God chose to bring light into our family through the person of Ron Dodds.

Chapter 4

Sutherland Springs

The year 1998 was a tough year in so many respects. We had been having trouble with my son. He had turned eighteen and was trying to sow his oats with a not-very-good crowd. His friends convinced him to move out of the house. I was heartbroken. I tried to speak with him, to no avail.

During this time, Ron worked for someone in the church who taught him the vocation of appraiser; eventually he took the exams and passed.

In June of 1998, Ron's mom, to whom he was very close, passed away. She had accepted the Lord several months earlier through our niece. Ron had witnessed to her, but it was my niece who showed her the light, and my mother-in-law became a different person. She was buried in Pennsylvania, which is where Ron was born.

So we planned a trip to Pennsylvania, and I fell in love with the area. His family lived in Bethlehem, Pennsylvania, which is a beautiful town with Moravian roots.

Ron's parents were from Pottsville. I was pleased to meet his Pennsylvania family. During that road trip, Ron became very sick. He had symptoms of diabetes and started taking insulin.

Once we got home to Texas, he had an idea that he wanted to buy land in the country and move there. We found acreage in a town southeast of San Antonio called Sutherland Springs. Yes, that Sutherland Springs that years later would have someone shoot up a Baptist church that we used to drive by all of the time.

When we moved to the area, we first bought ten acres. My sister purchased a trailer, and we lived with her until our home was built. Then, we purchased another ten acres. It was about forty-five minutes each way from San Antonio. I was still working for the investments company, but in 1999, we had a problem—the company was investigated for embezzlement.

In 1999, Ron kept having pain in his back and we had to change doctors. He left the endocrinologist and went to visit a physician's assistant (PA). The PA listened to his symptoms and asked him if he had ever had a sonogram.

When Ron said, "no," the PA scheduled the sonogram. Unfortunately, our worst fears materialized. He had a mass the size of a grapefruit on one of his adrenal glands. The surgeon removed it, but it had already spread so Ron had to undergo a round of chemo. He had non-Hodgkin's lymphoma.

The mass had affected his adrenal gland, causing the diabetic symptoms. The endocrinologist had misdiagnosed the disease. The lymphoma should have been caught a year before. The diabetes would plague him years later.

During May of 1999, Ron was in the hospital having surgery while I was trying to close on a new house.

Talk about stress! We did finally close on the home. Then, my company was temporarily shut down because of the embezzlement issue. The CPA firm that was hired to investigate the company called and asked me to come back to help them find assets. I would have my full pay and benefits, so at least I had a job again.

Ron had a hard time going through chemo. The chemo, administered via pills, made him very emotional. If you knew Ron, you would know that he was an extremely intelligent man. He had a saying: "Business is business." He had an amazing way of being able to detach himself from a particular problem in order to find a solution. He thought in a very logical way and was not an emotional kind of person, but the pills affected him.

He would call me at work and cry because of a sad commercial. His behavior was totally illogical. Of course, anyone who has been through cancer will tell you that the disease is a very illogical disease. Ron went through all the rounds of chemotherapy. The doctor was very pleased with how well he did, and she said that if it didn't come back in a couple of years, then he was cured.

I looked for other work because the atmosphere at the current work environment was depressing. I received offers from three other employers. I accepted one as a bank auditor but quickly realized that I had made a mistake.

The job required a lot of traveling, and Ron was still convalescing, so he needed me. I then accepted a job working for an oil company in October of 1999, and it turned out to be one of the best career moves I ever made.

My sister married Kenneth in 2000 and moved back to San Antonio.

Chapter 5

9/11/01

In 2001, Ron wanted to start my accounting business on the side. I had a full-time job, but he said that he would run the accounting company. Ron asked if he could read my Intermediate Accounting book one day and I said, "Go ahead."

After reading it, he knew accounting. I studied for years in college for accounting! That was the kind of person Ron was and the brain that he had. 2001 was actually a pretty good year for our finances and for travel.

In August, we visited Chicago and had a great time. In September, we went to visit his aunt and uncle in Bethlehem, Pennsylvania. We had such a blessed visit. We had bought tickets to travel by bus to New York City on September 10, 2001.

Up to this point, I had never visited NYC, and I had urged Ron for us to visit. However, the night before we were to leave, Ron had a very bad feeling about going to NYC. He felt that something bad would happen, perhaps being mugged. Throughout our marriage, I had learned to pay attention to his instincts. So we changed our flight plans to fly home on September 11. I remember keeping those two tickets; they are hidden in a box somewhere in my house.

We were supposed to fly from Baltimore Washington International Airport through Chicago O'Hare back to San Antonio. We arrived at Chicago O'Hare around 8:30 a.m. It's been more than twenty years, so I don't remember the exact time. I do remember that when we arrived, we had to deboard, which was unusual. Normally passengers are allowed to stay in their seats if they were continuing on the next flight. As we walked through the airport, none of the TVs were on. Ron immediately felt a sense of unease and said, "Something isn't right."

He called his dad in Florida, and his dad told him what happened. Ron said that he doubted if we would board the plane again. Just then, a little bar in the airport turned on a TV, and soon we all watched in disbelief as the second tower was hit. Everything became so surreal. Everyone who watched it started to cry.

At this point, the airport started the evacuation process. They told us to leave without our luggage, that they would send it to us. I thought, *We'll never see that luggage ever again.* Because we had just been in Chicago the previous month, we decided to head downtown where we had a free night's stay at the Embassy Suites.

We took a cab to the hotel and noticed that hordes of people were leaving downtown as we were heading toward it. I realized that everyone was leaving because, at this point, no one was sure what else was going to get hit, and Chicago has a lot of high-rise buildings.

We arrived at our hotel and went out for dinner. Many places had closed following the attacks. We finally found a restaurant that was open but empty. Everyone just wanted to talk about where they were when it happened. We, as a nation, were sad and mourning. We didn't know the people we were talking to, but we were all crying together.

After a couple of days in the hotel, Ron said that he didn't think the airports were going to open any time soon, so we probably needed to rent a car and drive back home. Rental cars were hard to come by, but we found one and headed south. We drove back twenty hours straight because we wanted to be with our family. As we drove past the Arch in St. Louis, it was darkened. Everything was a possible target for another attack.

We finally arrived home and went to the airport to get our car. Before 9/11, it was possible to park fairly close to the airport. Our car had been towed far from the airport, but we managed to find it. Airport staff said that they would call us when our luggage arrived.

We drove to our home in Sutherland Springs, and I remember being so happy that I was home. After about a week or so, the airport called us and said that they had our luggage and that we could pick it up. That was a nice surprise; I never thought that I would see it again.

9/11 was the saddest day ever in America. Ron and I would mourn it every year. We always watched all of the documentaries.

It is chilling to think that our airplane was in the air at the same time as the four fatal planes. God was watching over us and protecting us. This is what God does when you are in ministry and trying to do the right thing. The hand of God is upon you.

Chapter 6

Stem Cell Transplant

In 2002, while at the accounting business, Ron had an accident and broke his leg. I won't even go into details of what happened because it was actually a bit disturbing, but when he broke the leg, one of the lymph nodes in his neck became very swollen. The doctors were very concerned since he had been a cancer patient. Sure enough, our worst fears came to be. The doctor said that the lymphoma had recurred.

This time, they recommended that Ron go through a bone marrow transplant. The doctors were convinced that he would be cured with it. We looked for donors, but he was a hard match. None of his family qualified for a match so the doctors recommended that he undergo a stem cell transplant using his own stem cells as they were healthy.

Two of the things that I figured out in dealing with cancer is that no one responds the same way, and the doctors don't tell you everything that could happen. We went into this venture naive and just hoping to cure Ron's disease. What would happen next would change us forever.

I journaled my days during this period of my life because it definitely was one of the hardest phases of our lives. However, when I started writing this book, I searched high and low for the journal in order to document everything that happened to us, but to no avail. I figured that God wanted me to reach into my memory bank and put down the important things. I also felt that He wanted to guide me through the memories. This chapter will not be chronological because it occurred so many years ago, but I will share some of the things that I do remember.

First of all, Ron underwent the transplant at the Methodist Hospital in San Antonio because his oncologist was affiliated with that hospital. At that time, anyone undergoing a stem cell transplant would be transferred to a specific section of the hospital. That part of the hospital was old and not equipped for any handicapped patients.

If you recall, at this time, Ron was in a wheelchair because he had a broken leg that could not be operated on because he had cancer. Since Ron needed to be in a handicapped room, he was placed on the regular oncology floor, which was equipped for disabled patients.

Also, he had to transfer to a stem cell doctor. At that time, Dr. Paul Shaughnessy was the doctor who was handling the transplants. Dr. Shaughnessy was a former Air Force doctor, and he was excellent.

For anyone that has ever had to be in the hospital for any number of days, you learn to search for the "good" doctors and the "good" nurses because, unfortunately, they are not all equal. I learned that the oncology nurses and doctors are mostly very good because they deal with real life-and-death situations every day. We discovered that in a life-and-death situation, you bond with the people fighting the battle with you. Literally, you are in a war to cure cancer, and you are in the trenches with them. It is a daily battle, and it is certainly not for the faint of heart.

At that the time, the process for the stem cell transplant required that Ron had to receive whole body chemotherapy and radiation for a few days. During that time, the medical team harvested his good stem cells so that at a later point, they could reintroduce them back into his body. They basically take a body to a point of near death until it's neutropenic with decreased white blood cells and no immunity and then return the healthy stem cells back into the body.

After going through the whole process, I thought it was quite barbaric; I couldn't imagine a child or an elderly person going through it, but they do. Chemotherapy we had experienced, but Ron had never had radiation. The radiation caused terrible diarrhea, and I was the one that helped the nurse with Ron because he was so sick. The nurse could not keep up with him.

Ron already had a port for chemotherapy, but he needed a port for the actual stem cell transplant. So he eventually had two ports. Ron's transplant port became infected, so they had to add another port in his neck, which was very uncomfortable for him.

I always say that with Ron, everything that could go wrong always went wrong. I really do think that the enemy was always trying to kill him physically. I don't think he had good health to begin with, but some of the things that happened were hard to explain.

As the days wore on, I realized that Ron was not doing well, and I needed to be with him at the hospital full time. I took a leave of absence from my work at the oil company and stayed with him. We were still living in Sutherland Springs, and Dr. Shaughnessy told us that Ron had to be close to the hospital in San Antonio. We had to rent an apartment near the hospital, so I was paying for two homes.

I tried to go take care of our animals, but it became futile. I am so blessed to have a good family. I talked to my sister and my brother-in-law, who were living back in San Antonio, and they told me not to worry. They moved into our house in Sutherland Springs and commuted so they could take care of the house and our animals. Who does that? That is called love.

Ron was to have his stem cells reintroduced around Labor Day of 2002. He was getting too sick though, and the doctor would not let him leave the hospital and go to the apartment. He was becoming difficult to handle because of the side effects, and he couldn't walk.

The medical team decided to move him from the regular oncology ward to the stem cell ward because he would have a dedicated nurse there. However, the move was horrible for Ron. The small, claustrophobic room was not handicapped equipped. When it was time for him to receive his stem cells, he did not do well.

After they reintroduced his stem cells, he went back to his room, but he didn't eat for days. He didn't talk either. I'm sure he felt horrible, so I sat by his side. I decided to look up all the Scriptures that talked about healing, and I prayed them every day, hoping that God would hear my cry for help.

I so wanted Ron to live. I learned that in asking for healing, you have to have the faith that it will happen, so then I looked up Scriptures on faith, which led to Scriptures of hope. I want to compile them all someday and give them to people who need them (that's another project!).

Ron and I sat together and watched *SpongeBob* endlessly until one day, he started to talk again. His recovery was slow, but his eating patterns got better as the days went on. The whole process took about three months, but it should have been a lot shorter if he had not had so many problems.

It was such a tough time, but I know we were able to get through because we knew the Lord. I remember Ron telling people that he would see me at the edge of the bed praying and he would get mad. Then, the Lord softened his heart, and he was so grateful that he had a praying wife.

I know that many people go through tough times and similar situations, but I don't know how they survive without God. I am positive that He gave us the strength and the grace to get through all the hardships.

Chapter 7

Light at the End of the Tunnel

One day while in the hospital, Ron told me that he had epiphany with God while in the hospital. He had asked God to let him live because he wanted to see our son who was estranged at the time, and he wanted to make amends for how we had left our last church. God told him that everything Ron had done was for his own selfish gain and not for God's.

Ron repented and promised God that he would never waste another day without sharing the Gospel. Something inside him changed. I have no doubt that this was when Ron really found his calling.

He started sharing the Gospel with the nurses. Some nurses would bring other nurses. Our room would always have a bunch of people in it, which was very unusual for the transplant ward. We had to walk around with masks all the time because the patients all had low immune systems.

Dr. Shaughnessy told me how proud he was that I learned all of the medical jargon and all the medications—he said that I was like a nurse. I'm sure that's common for anyone that watches out for their loved one. Then one day, Dr. Shaughnessy said, "Ok, that's it." Ron would go back to the apartment and just come in for checkups. I looked at the doctor and said, "What are we supposed to do?" He said, "Yes, it's time to cut the cord."

I felt like my daddy was leaving me to go out into the cold, cruel world by myself. Everything was so surreal after the intense time that we had just gone through. Ron started eating little by little. I would make him egg salad sandwiches, and he lived off those sandwiches for a while.

We lived in the apartment for a couple more months while Ron recovered. One day we finally moved back to our house in Sutherland Springs. Strangely, it did not feel like home anymore. The following year in 2003, Ron found a good orthopedic surgeon who was able to fix his leg and, before you know it, Ron started walking again.

He had been in a wheelchair for almost a year. I distinctly remember when he told me that he didn't need the wheelchair anymore. He was becoming more independent again after long hard days of just the two of us, with me doing almost everything for him. It was an adjustment for me to see him not needing me again.

Ron started to trust my judgment, and our bond grew even stronger. He now knew that he could rely on me and that I would not fail him.

Chapter 8

More Miracles

Ron started working as an appraiser again. One day, he was going to work to meet with Isaac, who was now working in the same field. This was the same Isaac who had once been his student years before. He and Ron would remain friends for life. They were both running late that day and agreed that they would meet at a later time.

Ron was driving on a street called West Avenue, which was near his work. As he drove along, he saw our son standing in the parking lot and he decided to approach him. Dorian told him that he was waiting for a ride because his car was not working, so for a week Ron drove him to work.

Then, Dorian told him that he was ready to see me and to come back into our family. At the end of that week, Ron told me what had been happening. I was upset because he'd kept it from me, but Ron had the ability to do that. He could be very objective even with personal situations.

So, the three of us met for dinner at Saltgrass Steakhouse, as we wanted to be in a neutral place. When we got together, we could not even remember why he had left. It had been six years! I think I prayed for my son every single day during those six years. I asked the Lord to watch over him no matter what. Just like that, our son was back in our family.

He never moved back into our house, but he visited us in Sutherland Springs. He helped Ron mow the lawn. This was most assuredly a miracle and the Lord honored one of Ron's requests. It was no less a miracle than the fact that Ron had survived the stem cell transplant and all the infections.

Similarly, Ron and I started reading *The Purpose Driven Life* and doing the corresponding Bible study together. Ron called our previous church and scheduled a meeting.

During that meeting, again we couldn't remember why we left, so we rejoined our church and were back in ministry. When we returned, Isaac was the worship leader at the church. It seemed that all the students that Ron had at Youth Group were now in leadership. During this time, the doctors asked Ron to move closer to San Antonio so he would be close to a hospital in case anything happened.

Chapter 9

Rice Road

Ron went back to work appraising homes, and he found a home on the east side of San Antonio that had been built in 1936. It was the original home on what used to be a farm. The home was on an acre. So we downsized from twenty acres in the country to an acre in the middle of San Antonio. The neighborhood was not the best, but the home allowed for privacy, which is what Ron wanted.

When he first took me to the home, I almost cried. I had this huge, beautiful home in the country, and we were moving into this old house. Ron kept trying to describe to me how he was going to renovate it, and boy did it need it. We had to put in all new electricity because it had ancient electricity that could not handle all of the technology that Ron would bring in. Ron pulled up the carpet and we restored the original wooden floors. We spent most of the renovation in the kitchen because Ron loved to cook. A friend from church helped us with the renovation.

We sold the home in Sutherland Springs so quickly that we had to move into an apartment until our new home was finished.

The home had belonged to a German heritage family. The couple that lived behind us were the owners of this home. The man grew up in the home and his parents owned it when it was a farm.

Little did we know that these neighbors would become like family. The wife was old enough to be our mom and she was just like Ron. She reminded Ron of his mom who had passed away in 1998. I always find that God finds a way to restore what we need even if we don't know what we need.

On Mother's Day weekend of 2004, we moved into the house on Rice Road. It was a small house, but the front room was large and would allow for company. Ron worked from home, and an addition in the back of the house was satisfactory for his business.

I was still working at the oil company and making pretty good money. I had been promoted several times and was moving toward upper management.

One of the difficult decisions that we had to make was what animals we would bring from the country. Unfortunately, we couldn't bring them all. We brought Tex, our ranch dog; Pepper, our house dog; and Baldrick, our outdoor cat. I plan to write a book on their stories someday.

Our neighbor came over the one day and started to feed our animals. We would spend Sundays at their house just relaxing. She always kept such a beautiful home; it was good for our soul to spend time with them. They were both believers, and I think they were thankful that we were believers too.

One day, a little brown, reddish dog jumped into our yard, and Tex was about to attack it. Ron saved the little dog, and I tried to find a home for it. I'm pretty sure that it belonged to the neighbors across the street, but they mistreated her, so I didn't put a lot of effort into returning her to them.

She was with us a week and I found a home for her at work, but by this time Ron had become attached to her. We named her Chica, and, according to the vet, she was half Dachshund and half Chihuahua, so she was a Chiweenie. She turned out to be one of the best pets we have ever had. I think all of our pets were the best, but Chica and Ron just had a love fest.

Chapter 10

Number Three

Toward the end of 2004, Ron started showing signs that he was not well. He returned to his oncologist, and she confirmed that he had a third occurrence of lymphoma. The oncologist suggested that he undergo another bone marrow transplant, but the last one took such a toll on him physically that we said no.

Ron looked for other alternative methods and found a book by a doctor who wrote about a regimen that would cure cancer, so Ron started doing what that doctor recommended. He took time away from work again to lead a stress-free life. He started organic juicing every day, and he became a vegetarian for almost two years. We all prayed vehemently for Ron.

After about six months of this regimen, the doctors could not find cancer. His oncologist said that she was not sure what he was doing, but whatever it was to just continue because it looked like he was back in remission.

Again, this was a miracle from God. This method worked for Ron, but it might not work for everyone. If I were faced with cancer, I would try it and see if it helped. It just means being diligent. We were so focused on getting him better.

Of course, it took a lot of faith and in the end, it was God's healing touch on his body. I know that our life seemed like something was always happening to us, but through it Ron was always a light to others. He always had such a positive outlook that you never would have known what he was going through. He was a problem solver, so he was always trying to help people solve their problems.

He truly was an inspiration to others, and I think that God continued to honor him in return. I try to cite all of the miracles that God did for us because they were in everyday life. He will do the same for others, but you do have to be alert and look for them.

Chapter 11

Ministry

We went back to our old church, which was a Messianic Jewish church. Ron started a home study with Isaac, who as I mentioned was now the worship leader at our church. They both led a weekly home Bible study from the church. We served food, studied the Bible, and enjoyed fellowship. It was such a blessing. We had about twenty people attending at a time.

I realized that Isaac was a good Bible teacher. He was young, but he was so knowledgeable. I knew he was destined for great things. He and Ron worked so well together.

In the year 2005, I went with Ron on my very first trip to Israel. Ron had been there many times before with his prior ministry in Florida. It was an eye opener. Just like Ron, I fell in love with the land, the people, and the food. I remember staying up late at night reading the Bible regarding the places that I had just visited.

Ron met a very special pastor named Guy Cohen who would become one of his best friends. They were like brothers. He was a young pastor of a church. Ron would help him build ideas.

In 2006, while Ron and Isaac were in Israel for Isaac's first trip, Ron had another epiphany. Most of the ministries in Israel were sorely in need of a 501c3 organization that would help them gain donations from the US. Ron felt that we could be that conduit.

When he returned back to the States, we applied for 501c3 status, and that is how we started Spring of Hope. We started working with three to five ministries in Israel, and it became a blessing for us.

After a couple of years, Ron and Isaac knew they had something special together, so in 2009, they started a small church. We had all left the Messianic church, but this time we left it properly. We did it before the church, and the pastor blessed our endeavors going forward.

There were five of us leaders in this new endeavor. The new church was called Prince of Peace. We met at our house in the beginning. We had some friends who had a church on the south side of San Antonio. They offered their church to us on Friday evenings, which is when we had service. We were involved with this church for about a year.

Chapter 12

Olivet

During this time, Ron was still running our ministry, Spring of Hope. Ron and Pastor Guy from Israel went to minister at a church in Abbotsford, British Columbia, called Olivet Church. Guy was going to speak at that church, and Ron was his guide.

Ron called me that day and told me that the church was a former Mennonite Church. He said that he was sure that nothing would come of it because they were mostly German and probably did not mix well with the Messianic Jewish movement. Who could have guessed what would happen next?

Ron and Guy really connected with the then-pastor of that church, and that church really had a heart for Israel. Ron started traveling up there during 2008 and 2009. In 2009, the pastors invited Ron to lead a tour to Israel with some of the leaders of the church.

I went with them on this tour, and I learned new things about my husband. He was an amazing teacher.

He had such knowledge of the land, the history, and the spiritual aspects. I kept a journal, and I kept writing what he was teaching. I couldn't believe that was my husband. He was always surprising me with the depth of his being.

That year, there were problems at Olivet. Ron kept traveling up there, but we couldn't afford to do so. Ron bonded with Pastor Stacey who had replaced the main pastor. They had a very special friendship similar to Ron's relationship with Pastor Guy.

The travel and time there was expensive, plus he was spending valuable time away from our family. I prayed about this, and somehow the Lord impressed upon me that we should move up there. Ron continued to travel there for about a year, and I prayed about this the entire time.

One day, Ron approached me and said that he felt that the Lord was leading him to Abbotsford. I told him that the Lord had already spoken to me and that I was in agreement.

Mind you, I had never lived anywhere else but San Antonio and the surrounding area. Again, little did we know the adventure that we would embark on.

Chapter 13

Washington/Canada

On Labor Day weekend 2010, we made the move to what I always called Washington-Canada because we couldn't find housing in Canada, but we found a beautiful rental home in a town called Lynden, Washington, right across the border from Abbotsford, British Columbia. Ron volunteered full time at the church as the church administrator, and periodically he preached the main message.

The town of Lynden was a Dutch-settled community. It was in the Pacific Northwest, so everything was so green with flowers everywhere. We were smack in the middle of dairy farms. It was beautiful, but we definitely were outsiders.

All the locals were tall, beautiful people—and then there was us. The residents were nice enough, but we were not like them. From a career standpoint, in this part of the country, people and businesses didn't really need accountants. They needed bookkeepers, so I had a difficult time finding a decent-paying job.

Thank God that I had a healthy 401K that I had amassed from working at the oil company. We ended up practically living on it. I didn't know how the bills were paid, but God made it work every week.

I had never lived far from my family, so it was difficult for me. I couldn't find decent work. I didn't have any friends. Some days I would just cry myself to sleep because I was homesick. Plus, there was the time difference so I couldn't call my family whenever I wanted.

However, Ron loved his job, and he absolutely loved Olivet. He was totally sold on it. Pastor Stacey became the main pastor when we got there. He became ill, so Ron had to sub for him frequently during this time.

Ron was flourishing spiritually. Pastor Stacey was such a good influence on him. Ron was so smart, but he almost never spent any time preparing for messages. Pastor Stacey was equally smart, but he was so devoted to the Lord that he would spent upward of thirty hours preparing for one message. He shamed Ron into studying, but Ron became a better teacher for it.

As bad as I felt about my personal and work life, I too was growing spiritually by leaps and bounds. The church was very Bible-literate. They knew Scripture. If anyone taught out of line, the congregation called them on it. I learned that knowing the word of God is one of the most important things in our spiritual walk. I was on the praise team and on the nursery team.

Our worship leader was amazing. At this time, I began to have issues with acid reflux so I would periodically lose my voice. The worship leader asked me to be a part of the praise team, and I told her that I couldn't always sing because I didn't always have a voice. She told me that wasn't why she was asking. She said that she knew that I could worship, and that's what she needed on the team. There were days when I could only croak into the microphone, but somehow the Lord made it sound like music.

One day, I asked one of the music technicians what I sounded like, and he said I was fine. I think it was divine intervention. I remember sessions where we would be in service worshipping, and I could hear what sounded like a whole choir behind us, but we had only a small band. I realized that I was hearing angels singing with us. I would experience this again later in life.

This was the first time in my ministry walk that I actually sacrificed my comfort to leave everything I knew to follow the Lord. Although it was difficult, I would encourage anyone who is given the opportunity to do it if you can. Although it was not easy, it was one of the most rewarding times of my life. Literally, I felt as if it was us and the Lord walking through the journey. I grew spiritually, in faith and in the Word.

Chapter 14

What's Wrong?

I finally found a good job in Surrey, British Columbia, working for an American tax accountant doing taxes. It was very rewarding. He was teaching the team so much. Ron and I took a birthday vacation to New York City the summer of 2011, which was fabulous. I had never been to New York City. I loved it, and we had so much fun.

When we returned though, Ron developed a blood clot and was having health problems. I thought, *What am I going to do up here without family support if Ron gets sick again?* Once someone has cancer, the fear of a recurrence always looms. I begged Ron to go home to Texas, but he didn't want to leave because he was doing so well at the church.

I reached out to a mentor in San Antonio to see if she could find me work and she did. I flew to San Antonio for a job interview and was able to land a job, but the pay wasn't that great. For the first time in my life, I told Ron what we were going to do: We were leaving and returning home.

He couldn't argue because he was getting so sick. However, he was so heartbroken. Olivet was one of the best things that he had done in ministry. We had grown so close to all of our friends at the church. The day of our last service arrived. All of the leadership was on the stage to bless us and wish us well. Pastor Stacey could barely talk because he was crying so much. We all just cried up there.

It was so painful to leave, yet I knew in my heart that this was the only way. So, Ron and I drove the grueling three-day trip back to San Antonio. I had to drive most of the way because Ron was so ill. He was very despondent. He was not only sick; he was heartbroken.

In retrospect, I think we should have left, but I pushed it. I should have allowed Ron to make that decision. I've always regretted that we left too soon. Ron had always made the final decision in our marriage, and I ended up regretting my decision. I think I was afraid, and the fear caused me to push the move back to Texas.

Chapter 15

Return to Texas

I started working at my new job and instantly hated it. The woman who was training me was always looking to see where I didn't learn something and search for errors that I or my team had done. My direct boss was a bully. The only saving grace is that I met a young man named John who was a fellow supervisor, and we would meet later in life in a professional manner.

We arrived in San Antonio on October 12, 2011, and in December, Ron had his first heart attack. I could deal with cancer. I would say that I was an expert in the cancer arena, but a heart attack was uncharted waters.

The cardiologist told us that Ron had suffered a heart attack, but because of all the chemotherapy and radiation, Ron's arteries had shrunk, and the doctors could not perform bypass surgery. Most of his arteries were clogged, so at this point all they could do was send him home and eventually he would probably die.

This was devastating news. Not only was I living with the guilt that maybe I had caused the heart attack because he was so heartbroken leaving Canada, but now he was probably going to die.

The days passed and Ron just sat in his recliner. He ate and drank, but he was not himself. He was always such a positive person, but I'm sure he didn't feel well. We had no church and now no friends because we had left Canada.

Eventually, I decided to form a small prayer group that would meet at my house. I had a small group of women friends who would meet just to lift our prayers to the Lord. I invited Ron to join us. He slowly but surely started engaging. He decided to teach some Bible study at our "prayer" group. We were calling ourselves the "Prayer Chicks."

Ron didn't die. He found a good cardiologist through another friend of ours and the doctor told him that he could treat him with medication.

I think that sometimes in life and in ministry, you just have to wait on the Lord. I truly regretted returning to San Antonio and I felt that I had made a grave error and that I was paying for it, but God does not work that way. You just have to keep going and having faith that God has your life under control no matter what obstacles life brings you.

Chapter 16

Woodridge Oaks

We lived at our rental home on Woodridge Oaks from 2011 to 2014. I quit my new job that I moved to Texas for because it became unbearable, and I floundered for a while. I did some consulting, which I hated because I was not part of a team.

A ministry friend of ours contacted me one day, and he said that he had an accountant position, so he encouraged me to apply. The company was owned by a Christian billionaire who lived in San Antonio, and he led his company in a Christian manner. I think at the time, it was what I needed.

Our friend Isaac became an Anglican priest and served in New Braunfels. We attended his church a few times, including during his wedding. Ron and Isaac had remained friends through the years and throughout our wanderings. He was young enough to be our son, but he filled many roles.

He had worked for us at the appraisal business as well. Now, Father Isaac had the appraisal business and asked Ron if he could help him. The tables had turned. Ron was now the employee instead of the owner. I didn't care as long as he was interested in something.

We continued our prayer/Bible study group for a while. I eventually left the Christian company and went to work for the City of San Antonio. I worked downtown and loved it, but it paid little. If I had joined the City when I was young, benefits would have been great.

Our son married around this time, and we were so happy that he had found someone.

The thing that amazed me about this time period is that Ron had such a will to live. His body had gone through so much, yet he had so much to give. Through it all, Ron never lost faith. He gave all that he had until the very end, and the Lord was faithful.

Chapter 17

Fairford (Manor)

In 2014, Ron told me that he wanted to buy a house for me again. We had been renting at Woodridge Oaks. He said that he wanted to leave something for me if and when the Lord took him. He miraculously recovered from the heart attack. He had an excellent cardiologist who understood his pathology and worked with him.

Father Isaac left the church in New Braunfels, and then landed a position as Assistant Rector at a church in San Antonio. He invited us to visit.

I grew up Catholic, so I was not really interested in attending a denominational church. However, Ron started attending on Sundays and in May of 2014, he invited me to attend church because he was getting "confirmed." I said, "What!?" I had to attend because I wanted to know what kind of a church this was.

I attended that service, and the existing Rector approached me and said that he heard that I was a "vocalist." I said, "No, Father. I'm not a vocalist, but if you need someone who worships the Lord, then I am that person." At this time, they had a contemporary worship service called Koinonia. I joined the worship team, and I never left the church. Ron eventually served as the Junior Warden, then later as a Treasurer. We were happy there at the time.

Ron found a home for me on a street called Fairford Drive and we moved in. The amazing thing is that the initial owners of this home were originally from Pennsylvania, Ron's home state. They had a son who died from cancer the day after he graduated from high school. Ron had experienced cancer.

The home needed little updating, and so we lived there. This home became a refuge for both Ron and me. In December of 2014, there was a dog that had been running around the neighborhood. People were feeding him, but no one was taking him in. All of our pets had always loved Ron more, although I fed them and cleaned their litter box or took them out. Ron would tease me that someday I should get my own pet that would love me.

I took in that dog on a cold December day because I was concerned for him. At the time, we had Chica, the chiweenie, and she was the princess of the household. I brought in this dog wondering if he would get along with Chica. Chica was very hyper, but this dog was very calm. He became my shadow. I took him to the vet, and the vet said that he was full blooded rat terrier. I named him Lord Wishbone because he was so upright and stately that I thought that his dog voice had a British accent. He became Lord Wishbone of Fairford Manor.

During this time, our son decided to divorce his wife. This was very upsetting for us because it was not just a divorce of two people, but a divorce of two families. Ron and I cried because we loved our daughter-in-law. It was a very sad time in our lives. We hoped that they would come to their senses but to no avail.

They would not go to counseling and so it was over. For a few months, I did not speak to my son because I was so disappointed. In April of 2015, I finally called Dorian because I couldn't continue to not have a relationship with my own son. We had gone through that before. After all, he was my son whether I agreed with his decisions or not.

Also, at this time, I changed jobs yet again to work with my friend, John. The company was a global generic soda company. I loved it. My friend and I were a great team. I had a team of twelve associates and a supervisor. The supervisor and I became friends, and we did great things at that company.

It seemed like life was back on track because we found a church and I had a stable job.

Chapter 18

The Beginning of the End

Ron and I continued to serve at the Anglican church. On Fridays, the priest had a band of excellent musicians, and we had a contemporary worship service in the evenings. Ron served on the music board, and I served as a singer. We had fun. I was doing well at my current job and things seem to be normal for a while.

In early 2016, I was returning from a conference in Houston with John, when I received a phone call from Ron that he fell while he was at home, and he thought that he had broken his knee cap.

I returned home as soon as I could, and we rushed him to the hospital. It was just as he suspected—he'd broken his patella straight across. A great surgeon performed the surgery to restore his knee, but the issue now was how Ron would get around. He was a big guy, and I was not able to help him.

A nurse at the hospital convinced me to admit him to a rehabilitation facility near the house. Ron was there for almost a week, but he was very concerned. He said that the care at that facility was less than stellar, and he had trouble especially at night. On the Thursday a week after the surgery, Ron needed help, and a certified nursing assistant did not follow the proper protocol of using a belt to lift him up.

She let him fall on the bed, and she fell on him—right on the broken patella. This time the patella broke on the top into seven pieces. The surgeon had to redo the surgery. This time the hospital kept him in rehabilitation there at the hospital.

Ron eventually was able to walk again, but once he returned home, he was so afraid of falling again that he seldom left the wheelchair. We moved his bedroom to his office and purchased a medical bed so it would be easier for him to get in and out of the bed. It became the new normal to just pack his wheelchair. He was able to drive, but it became more and more limited.

As difficult a time as this was, Ron continued to serve in leadership at church. He was faithful to continue attending services. He loved church and did not want to let anyone down. The Lord was faithful and gave Ron the strength to continue in ministry.

Chapter 19

The Challenges of Ministry

In 2017, we were happy attending the Anglican church, and we were both in leadership. If you have been in leadership, you know that leadership comes with its own hazards. Those in leadership know the intimate details of what is happening in the church.

This was not our first rodeo, but we allowed things to play out. Another thing we learned in leadership is that you don't try to sway others to your view. Eventually, the truth always plays itself out, and so it happened at this little church.

I will not go into all of the sordid details. Suffice it to say that some very painful things occurred at the church, and it took a toll on Ron's health. I begged him for us to just leave the church, but he would not have it. As you remember, Father Isaac was the associate pastor of this church, and Ron would not think of leaving him. Ron was always loyal to a fault, and he always did what he was convinced was the right thing.

Ron, who was an extremely intelligent man, started falling asleep in midsentence. I knew something was very wrong. Ron was diabetic, and the doctors were trying to keep him from going on dialysis. He had an incident where he was in the hospital for an experimental procedure, and he ended up Code Blue.

I knew something was very wrong when the chaplain was brought into the room, and he asked me if I was all right. I told him I was fine, and he told me that he was there for me! Ron eventually recovered, but it was yet another scary moment.

In May of that year, the doctors told him that his kidneys were failing and that he would have to go on dialysis. Again, a new term that we would eventually become experts in. We knew nothing of what that meant nor what it would entail so we went into it whole-heartedly, not fully understanding until later. Ron went into the clinic for treatment three times per week for two to four hours at a time.

By this point, I was working for a company in Boerne with the title of accounting manager, but the job was really a glorified bookkeeper position. I was miserable there. My direct supervisor was abusive. He was like a spoiled child when he didn't get his way.

Since I worked during the day, friends from the church agreed to drive Ron to his dialysis appointments. I was so grateful. There were so many people who loved Ron and would do just about anything for him. Ron tried to drive himself to the appointments in the beginning, but after treatment he was exhausted because his blood pressure went down during dialysis. Driving was not safe for him, so we set up the appointed rides. This routine went on through September of 2017.

In looking back at this period, I realize that God was right there. He put the right people in our lives at that time so Ron could attend his dialysis appointments. Never doubt that God is in the midst of difficulties. The Lord cares about every aspect of your life.

Chapter 20

Joy and Sadness

Luckily, the dialysis clinic was very close to our home on Fairford. Imagine that! God thought of all aspects of what we would need. Ron went in for his temporary port. As usual, the surgery was difficult because Ron had small veins from all the chemo and radiation that he had taken in the early 2000s. The doctor admitted him to the hospital for three days around Memorial Day weekend for his first dialysis treatment.

At this point, Ron was very sick, and the doctor wanted to keep a close eye on him. The nurses were great, and Ron was able to tolerate the dialysis. After this, he checked into the clinic by our house three days a week for four hours each day.

The treatment lowered his blood pressure so much that on some days the dialysis staff couldn't take as much water/waste as they needed too. Dialysis is not for the faint of heart. Those who have endured it or know someone who has endured it know that it comes with many risks and challenges. The odds seemed to be stacking up against Ron.

Ron had a strong will to live so he just kept on going no matter how hard it was getting. Again, the Lord provided the necessary medical personnel so we could get through this period.

Chapter 21

Issues of the Heart

The surgeries to put in a port and all the dialysis put a strain on Ron's heart. In September of 2017, Ron couldn't breathe, and I had to call an ambulance yet again to our home. He was rushed to the hospital and our worst nightmares were confirmed. Ron had suffered another heart attack. The doctors said that he had to undergo bypass surgery. They told us that the surgery was risky because of his shrunken veins.

They found a heart surgeon who was willing to take the case. He was an expert in his field and had been around for a long time.

We had one day to make up our minds if he wanted the surgery or if we were ready to give up. I called our friends to meet us at the hospital because I wasn't sure what decision Ron would make. He decided to undergo the surgery but neither of us thought that he would survive it. Ron and I cried so much that day because we had to say our goodbyes—just in case. It was such a painful decision.

As usual, Ron gave me practical advice on what to do with our home and our businesses. Our friends and family waited through the night to see if he would survive. A nurse called me every hour to tell me how and what they were doing at each stage of the surgery. Every time the phone rang, I feared they were calling to tell me that he didn't make it. The surgery took five hours, then finally the surgeon came out to talk to me.

He said that he had never known anyone with such a desire to live. It reminded me of *The Princess Bride* (which was Ron's favorite movie) where Dread Pirate Roberts was asked, "What do you have to live for?" and he answered, "True love!"

That was the essence of Ron. He was a fighter and not a quitter. He would fight until the end. The surgeon said that he felt that he would make it. Ron went into the Intensive Care Unit (ICU) and stayed there for three weeks. It was excruciating.

They put him in a medically induced coma because he was intubated. I took turns with friends watching over him. I was still working at a place that I hated but didn't have a choice. I was so grateful for our family and friends who helped me during this time.

One day, Ron woke up, and the doctors started to wean him off all the machines. When Ron woke up, he was not himself. He was talking gibberish, and I thought that his brain was not right. The nurses assured me that it was from having been sedated for so long and that it would eventually wear off. This is very common with patients that have been under for so long.

Every day I went to the hospital, and we watched TV. One day, my sister and I were arguing over a show that we couldn't remember the name of, and Ron corrected us. That's when I knew that he would be okay. His senses came back, including his amazing brain.

Again, God answered our prayers. I prayed so hard during this time because I just was not ready to let go. It was yet another miracle that Ron survived the surgery. Later, I would find out why God spared his life.

Chapter 22

Another Miracle

By this time, my son was remarried and my then daughter-in-law was having a baby in another hospital. The baby was born on Rosh Hashanah of 2017. Rosh Hashanah is the Jewish New Year and a great time of celebration. The baby's sugars were low when he was born, so he was transferred to NICU. Seeing my grandson with all those wires and looking so tiny and helpless, I fell in love with him right away. I often went in and just held him.

Ezra was our first grandchild, and I discovered that the love for a grandchild is a different kind of love. It was different from the love I had for my own son, but it was love just the same.

Ezra eventually came out of the hospital, and one day his mother snuck him into ICU to see Ron. I still have the photo of their first meeting. Afterward when Ron came out of the hospital, he would just hold our grandson with a look of awe that Ezra was our flesh and blood. It was instant love, and I know that even though our grandson was still too little to know it, he loved Ron back.

Three weeks after surgery, Ron was moved to the physical therapy ward. All of the nurses cheered him on. That's the kind of person he was. He always had an impact on others, and they wished him nothing but the best. Ron started his rehabilitation.

Our pastor friend from Israel, Guy Cohen, came to visit him, and they were able to spend quality time together. Ron was back working in ministry from the hospital. At the time, he was the Junior Warden and became the Treasurer of the Anglican church while at the hospital.

Ron was in physical therapy for two months and was able to go home right before Thanksgiving of 2017. His sister, brother-in-law, and nephew from Atlanta came to visit us that Thanksgiving. Ron was still in his wheelchair, but his mind was sharp, and he was stronger than I had ever seen him up to that point considering all of the challenges of dialysis. I thought, *Well, I guess he's going to make it after all.* We had a great Thanksgiving that year.

Chapter 23

Winter is Here

December of 2017 was the worst season for the flu in Texas. Ron continued to go to dialysis, and on one of those visits, he contracted the flu. Ron was always susceptible to bronchitis every season, but this year it was the flu. He not only contracted one strain of the flu, but two strains! He was sick in December, continuing into January.

In January, I contracted one strain of the flu, and it put me on my back. I was ill for at least three days, and I couldn't shake the fever. I remember lying on the couch in the family room, feeling so bad that I couldn't tend to Ron, but I just couldn't. My work supervisor was very upset that I was out, but there is no way I could have worked.

Ron called me from his dialysis clinic on a Tuesday in January and told me that he couldn't breathe because of the flu. I told him to call the ambulance to have them pick him up from the clinic because he was so sick, and I couldn't help him. He went to the hospital.

I was still very sick and weak but on Wednesday, I decided to go to work with a fever because the office kept calling me. I went to the hospital after work to see how Ron was doing. He was in the ICU, and the doctor told me that that he had been very close to intubating him but wanted to give him a chance. Ron was able to make it out of ICU and into a room, but he was very weak.

I hoped that the doctors would send him to rehab, but we encountered obstacles. One of the doctors refused rehab for him, and she did everything possible so that we had no choice but to take him home.

That hospital and that particular doctor gave up on him— and even though he was not strong and not well, they sent him home. Unfortunately, sometimes the doctors and hospitals give up on patients. They don't want more work for themselves, and they make decisions for patients without giving them a choice.

I was so upset and kept thinking, *How in the world am I going to care for him and continue to work full time?* It was a terrible period, but it was time to make drastic decisions. Of course, all of this occurred prior to COVID.

Chapter 24

The End is Coming

In February of 2018, Ron was sent home without any physical therapy, but he was so weak from having been in the hospital that he could not walk. I had no choice but to quit my job. Continue to work for a job where I was unhappy or care for my husband? It was a no brainer for me, although Ron did not want me to quit.

I had not really told him everything that was happening at work because he had been so sick and was just trying to survive. Once I explained what was happening with my boss, then he finally agreed with me. I walked into the office, typed up my resignation letter, and dropped off the keys. I never looked back.

Since Ron was unable to walk, we had to call a medical equipment company to deliver equipment to our home. Ron's insurance agreed to pay for an ambulance to transfer him from our home to the dialysis clinic three times a week. The ambulance techs could not get to his bedroom in the back of the house, so Ron suggested we turn our formal living room into his bedroom.

I moved furniture around and moved his hospital bed into the living room, which became for all intents and purposes a hospital room. The ambulance techs were able to easily transport him from our home to the dialysis clinic. I needed a lift to help Ron get out of bed. He was a big man at the time, and I could not carry him to the bathroom, so the next thing was to order a commode.

Ron had so many medical appointments, including physical therapy at our home, that I bought a notebook and a Surface computer to keep track of everything he had to do each day. It was a full-time job keeping track of all the doctors' appointments, physical therapy appointments, dialysis appointments, and equipment that needed to be delivered.

Ron was on oxygen, which is normally not an issue for normal, walking people. The side effect of oxygen is CO_2, which can accumulate in the brain. CO_2 is generally released through the body when the individual walks.

However, Ron was bed-bound and could not extricate the CO_2. It started accumulating in his brain, putting him into an almost-comatose state. I hadn't expected this and didn't know how to deal with it.

The next few months were made up of Ron being normal for three weeks, then having issues with the CO_2 and having to go into the hospital. It happened every month like clockwork. In March or April, a doctor realized what was happening with the CO_2 and figured out that Ron needed to be on a Continuous Positive Airway Pressure machine (CPAP) that would help extricate the CO_2.

The CPAP was a whole other ball game. He had to wear a mask at night and breathe through this contraption. Ron was already claustrophobic, so this was probably one of the worst things that could happen to him. He also suffered from insomnia, so he was hardly sleeping. We had moved the sofa into what had been the dining room, and I slept there to be close if he needed to remove the CPAP.

God had given Ron a strong, beautiful voice for preaching. It was gone now due to the weeks that he had been intubated in ICU for the heart surgery. I finally moved back to our bedroom, but Ron was still in the living room. I told him to call me on my cell phone if he needed me. Otherwise I couldn't hear him because his voice was so hoarse. It was all so surreal.

Chapter 25

Still Fighting

In May of 2018, Ron again became ill and had to go to the hospital. Since the incident at the hospital in February when the doctors gave up on him, I moved him to a downtown hospital that I felt could deal with his complicated pathology. I found a doctor who had treated him before and had Ron's best interest at heart.

When Prince Harry got married that May, I got up super early in the morning and drove to the hospital to watch the wedding in Ron's room. Ron was not awake. That week, the doctors told me to bring my family in to meet with them. They talked to us about hospice and expressed that Ron was not doing well.

I didn't want to give up yet. Miraculously after three days treatment, Ron woke up. I told Ron what the doctors had said, and I asked him what he wanted to do. Ron was never a quitter, and he told me that he was not ready to die. So I told the doctors that as long as he was fighting, then I was right there with him. They released him and we went home. He was fine for another three weeks.

Chapter 26

Sleeping

Ron seemed to do so well in June. He still was weak, but he was trying so hard. The doctors and the therapists came to the house on schedule. Ron seemed to not be able to finish his physical therapy. I was concerned because Ron was such a fighter, but his body was starting to fail him. The last Monday of June, he went to dialysis like normal. He was in good spirits. I usually took a nap while he was out because he left at 5:30 in the morning.

When the ambulance brought him home, he was not awake. I knew there was something wrong. I asked them what happened, but they said that when they picked him up, he was sleeping. At the usual hour, his nurse came. His nurse had been in special forces, and he and Ron had a special bond. Like so many of Ron's caretakers, his nurse loved him. The nurse tried really hard to wake Ron, but I knew what the problem was. The CO_2 had accumulated in his brain again, and Ron was in a sort of coma.

The nurse was so diligent and worked on Ron for a couple of hours. Finally, the nurse turned to me and said, "If he doesn't wake up in the next couple of hours, you are going to have to take him to the hospital." I somehow felt in the pit of my stomach that if I took him to the hospital, I would never see him again. I waited and waited.

Around 6:30 p.m., I finally called the ambulance. I wanted them to take Ron to the downtown hospital I had chosen. We lived very close to the Medical Center. The ambulance drivers argued with me that their job was to take him to the closest hospital because he was not responsive. I argued that I wanted him at the hospital where I knew he could get the best treatment.

They finally called their supervisor, Dr. Brown. Dr. Brown explained that they needed to take him to the nearest hospital because he needed to get treatment as quickly as possible. I argued that we had already wasted precious time and that they could have already taken him downtown. Dr. Brown sighed and said, "Let me talk to the techs." They took him to the downtown hospital, and I followed the ambulance as I had done so many times before.

Chapter 27

Almost the End

I don't think Ron was conscious the rest of that week. We went in on a Monday evening, and like all the other times, I figured he would snap out of it on the third day. That had been our cycle. I was with him most of the days, and I had a couple of friends who stayed with him at night or early in the morning so I could go home and shower. I can't remember how long he was in ICU, but he was moved at some point.

He received an elderly friend from church on Monday night, and he told the nurse that she needed to leave. I think she was talking too much. At this point, Ron was fighting for his life. By Wednesday, I knew he wasn't doing well. He was still on dialysis, but he didn't seem to be fully awake. He didn't talk, and he struggled to breathe.

I knew that if anyone wanted to see him, they needed to visit him on Thursday or Friday. Through social media, I made a request for visitors. Little did I know that on

Thursday, he would have a stream of visitors from past ministries. Pastor Stacey from Abbotsford, British Columbia, was supposed to come the first week of July. At home, I tried to prepare for his visit when I could, but mostly I was at the hospital.

Ron had so many visitors that it became uncomfortable in the small ICU area and the hospital asked me to move him. The doctors finally talked to me and said that he wasn't responding and that I had to consider putting him in hospice.

Truly, I did not want to make that decision. I asked them to wait one more day to see if he would respond. Friday came and Ron was still not responding. Around lunch, I signed the paperwork to move him to hospice.

I cried and cried, but family and friends were with me. Once paperwork to enter hospice is signed, active treatment, including dialysis, is discontinued. I was eating lunch in the cafeteria with friends and family waiting for a room for Ron when the dialysis doctor called me.

She said that she had talked to Ron and asked him if he wanted dialysis that day and he shook his head no. She assured me that I had made the right decision. She and I both cried on the phone. Most people that really knew Ron knew his heart, and they loved him for it. They knew that he would not quit easily, and they all felt bad that things were going this way.

Chapter 28

The End

This is the hardest chapter I've had to write. Having to relive the last hours of my husband's life is excruciating to my heart. What I write, though, is not for me nor even for Ron. This was our story of what God did for us and how much He loved us and of all the miracles that we witnessed.

The doctors moved Ron to the hospice floor. He was not on dialysis, but he was on some oxygen to make him comfortable. He was not awake, but I could tell that he knew something had changed. The look on his face indicated he was in some discomfort.

Ron loved music so instinctively, I put on his earphones and turned on the music on his iPad. That seemed to help a little. I talked to him and held him a lot. I cried a lot too. I don't think that I understood what was happening. We must have had twenty people in the room. Some were friends and others were family. I remember bits and pieces of the people who were there.

Ron was moved around 4:00 p.m. on Friday, June 29, 2018. At around 5:00 p.m., Father Isaac came in. He said that we were going to read the Psalms, and his words were soothing. Father Isaac had with him an iPad that had some Irish hymns. He was very talented musically. Ron had Irish blood on his dad's side. Father Isaac started to sing Irish hymns. They were so beautiful.

At once, I saw Ron's countenance turn peaceful from the top of his head down to his feet. I heard other voices singing, and I've heard this before in worship. I looked up because I knew that no one would have known the lyrics that Father Isaac was singing. I realized that I was hearing angels singing.

In retrospect, I think at that hour, Ron's spirit left his body. I don't know if Father Isaac even realized what was happening, but he was one of Ron's best friends. It was so appropriate that it would be Father Isaac to help Ron's spirit go to heaven.

Father Isaac then left, and my family and I noticed that Ron's body was starting to turn cold. We mentioned that we did not think that he was there anymore. This was just a body starting to decay. People came and went, then they started to leave as it grew late. At some point, my brother-in-law went to get dinner for us from one of his family's restaurants downtown. It was Chinese. I think I ate.

My brother-in-law became very ill and had to leave, but my sister stayed. By 1:00 a.m. in the morning, most people had already left. A church friend was there, one of my friends was there, and my sister was there. Our church friend walked outside to walk his daughter to the car. As soon as he stepped outside, Ron took his last breath. It was almost as if he had waited all this time to just have the three of us there—my friend, my sister, and myself.

When our church friend walked back in after a few minutes, he figured out what happened. I was crying uncontrollably. When Ron took his last breath, I felt as if part of my heart was wrenched from my body. Truly, we were one, but now I felt alone for the first time in twenty-five years.

Our church friend said that he would stay until the coroner picked up the body. My sister and my friend walked me to my car and my sister offered to stay at my house overnight. She ended up staying with me for two weeks, and it was such a blessing.

As I drove out on Main Street from downtown, I called Ron's sister. She picked up the phone and we both just bawled. She knew why I was calling. I cried all night long. When my sister and I got home, we talked and cried. It was almost as if we couldn't sleep. June 30, 2018, was the saddest day of my life.

When I walked into our home, it felt totally empty. I knew in my heart and without a doubt that Ron was with the Lord. His spirit was no longer here. Ron deserved to be in heaven. He was such an evangelist. He shared Jesus with anyone who walked in his path. He was a righteous man and walked blameless before the Lord. Had it not been for Ron's faithfulness, my family would not have known the Lord. I am so thankful and grateful that Ron was in my life. I consider it an honor that God allowed me to be his wife here on earth. I truly don't deserve that honor. My husband was a man of God. I loved him while he was here, and I will always love him. I know without a doubt that he loved me.

I am so blessed that we lived our life and that God chose us for ministry, flawed as we were. Thank you, God, for Ron and for his life. I pray that our lives will tell Your story. All of our lives were just a testimony to what You continue to do on earth, and You still create miracles. We just have to look for them. I will never be the same, but I am blessed to live this life.

After Ron's death, life was so uncertain. I didn't know how I was going to live my life without him. A friend gave me a card in which she wrote that our lives are like a book and sometimes the chapters end. In this case, this chapter of my life that lasted for twenty-five years ended, but a new chapter will begin. What that chapter would be like I had no idea, but I did not have a choice in the matter. I would have to trust that God knew what He was doing and that His timing would be the right timing.

Chapter 29

Legacy

I now have a whole new story to tell, but that story does not involve Ron. It's just me and what I went through after he passed. I have stated why I wrote this book, which was to give glory to God for everything He did for us in this life. I intimately understand the importance of Ron's life and everything he did in the Kingdom for God. I also understand that I am very blessed to have been a part of it.

Another reason for writing this book was to tell the story of an extraordinary man and how he loved God so much that he lived his life in such a way as to give all glory to God.

I've said this before, and I'll say it again: Ron was not perfect by any means, and he was not always the easiest man to live with, but he had heart, and he had tenacity in the face of adversity. I've never known anyone like him. He always made such an impact on others that even strangers always remembered him. He left legacies in the form of the people that he influenced.

Father Isaac went on to lead a successful Anglican church that is now thriving. Pastor Stacey leads a successful church in Canada. Our own son, Dorian, is a successful businessman. I just don't know if they all would have been as successful if they had not been influenced by Ron.

I, myself, have gone on to be a successful businesswoman by myself because of everything that he taught me. I am not only blessed to have been chosen to be his wife, but just to have known him. I don't know if I will ever meet anyone else like him, but I know that it was a privilege. I am sure that he made an impact in Israel with the pastors that he worked with there. I just thank God every day that I have led this life, which was not always easy, but it was definitely amazing.

Epilogue

I hope that after reading *Our Story with God* that you all will take tidbits of what ministry life is like. It is not always easy, but it is so rewarding to walk with the Lord and know that what you are doing has impact. My job in life was to allow Ron to be as successful as he could in ministry. His job in life was to do what God asked him to do and to share Christ with as many people as he could.

I thought about leaving the part of his death out from the book, but this is real life, and life is not perfect. However, even at the end I could see God's hand on Ron's life and continued miracles. You have to look for the miracles because they are not always obvious. I have learned to look for inspiration wherever I can find it because God lets us know He is still with us. My prayer is that this book will be an inspiration to anyone who reads it.

Not everyone can be an evangelist like Ron or start a foundation like Spring of Hope. But all of us have a calling to share the Gospel with those around us. If we want to spend eternity with our loved ones, we need to ensure they know about the Lord. The Holy Spirit will work on their hearts, but our job is to share what the Lord has done for us and show His love in the way we live our lives. If we do, we will see miracles and blessings. What the Lord did for us, He will do for you.

A Note about Spring of Hope Foundation

Spring of Hope Foundation is a 501c3 foundation that works with believing pastors in Israel. We do not take any administrative fees and 100 percent of the funds go to the pastors. We have been blessed because Ron and I both had good jobs throughout our careers, and we were able to fund the ministry. The ministries that we work with in Israel are legitimate ministries and have all made an impact in their respective areas.

It is illegal to evangelize in Israel, and Spring of Hope is trying to save Jews, who are God's first people, by facilitating the churches in leading them to Christ.

This ministry was given to Ron by the Lord. It has blessed us immensely and we made some wonderful lifetime relationships. We have been so blessed by blessing the people of Israel.

Not everyone can be an evangelist like Ron and not everyone has his giftings, but you can contribute to the Kingdom with whatever the Lord has blessed you with. Watch and hear for the Lord's calling in your life.

He will bless you in ways you didn't think possible. Of course, I still miss Ron, and my next book will cover that next period of my life. However, I would do all of this over again knowing everything the Lord has shown me.

www.ingramcontent.com/pod-product-compliance
Lightning Source LLC
Chambersburg PA
CBHW032146040426
42449CB00005B/420